AF147543

Contents

Welcome

1 Write. Who are they?

Gizmo   ~~Hector Frost~~   Mike   Polly   Polly's mum   Smith   the Queen of Ice Island

1 Hector Frost

2 _____

3 _____

4 _____

5 _____

6 _____

7 _____

2 Look at Activity 1 and number the sentences.

a   He's wearing boots and a hat.   `4`

b   He's tall and thin. He likes diamonds and dogs.

c   He hasn't got any hair. He likes driving a skidoo.

d   She's got a diamond necklace.

e   She's got long black hair. She's wearing a dress.

f   He's black and white. He's wearing a green scarf around his neck.

g   She's got a daughter.

3 Look and tick (✓).

1 What does Polly hear?

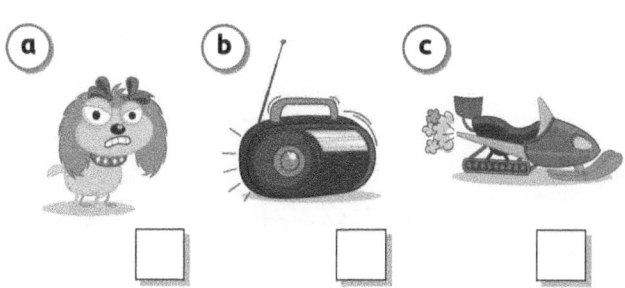

2 Who gets the diamonds?

4 Read and answer. *True* or *false*?

1	Polly wakes up in the middle of the night.	(True) / False
2	A red ribbon falls off the skidoo outside Polly's home.	True / False
3	Polly's mum asks the children to read the newspapers.	True / False
4	Polly's name is Polly Jones.	True / False
5	The diamonds are in the town.	True / False
6	The thieves steal the diamonds in the day.	True / False

5  Listen and match. Then write.

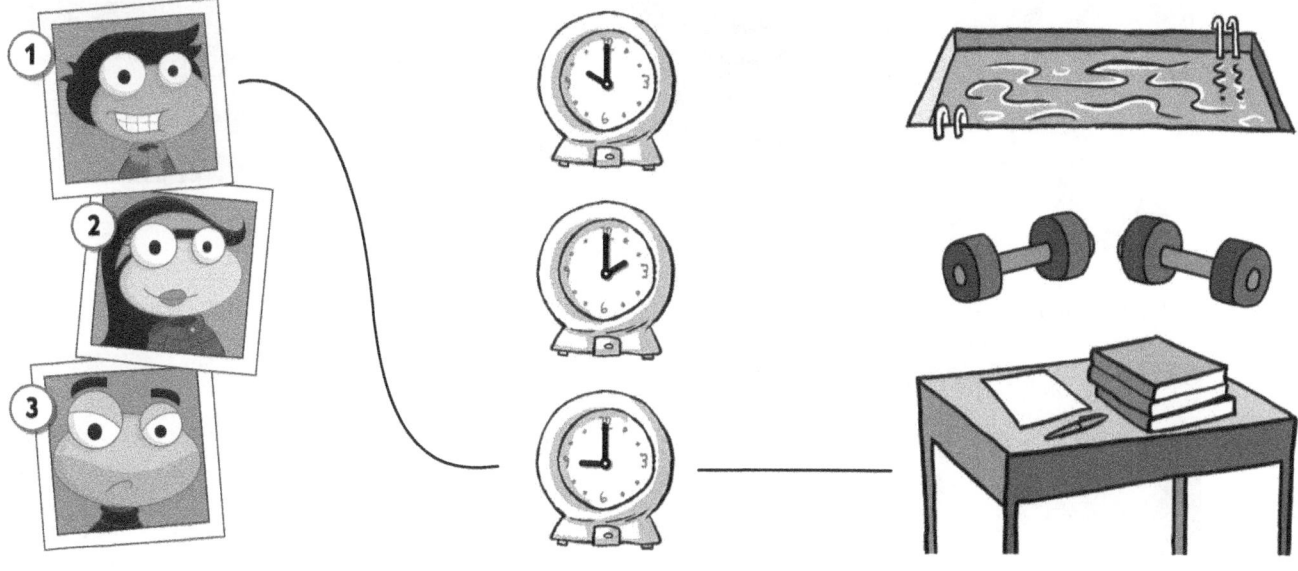

1 What's Mike doing?   <u>studying</u>

2 What's Polly doing?   _____

3 What's Smith doing?   _____

1 Friends

1 Find and circle six words.

df cute xeistraightodgood-lookingswospikyubaldcmibeautifulpac

2 Write. Use words from Activity 1.

1 I'm ___beautiful___ .

Emma

2 I've got _____ hair.

Maddy

3 I've got _____ hair.

Robbie

4 I'm _____ .

Dan

3 Find and write the questions.

1 (does) (look) (what) (she) (like) <u>What does she look like?</u>

2 (look) (what) (do) (like) (they) _____

3 (look) (does) (he) (what) (like) _____

4 Read and choose. Then look and tick (✓) the true sentences.

a

1 He ((is) / has got) bald.   ✓

2 He (is / has got) long, straight hair.   ☐

b

1 She (has got / is) beautiful.   ☐

2 She (has got / is) glasses.   ☐

c

1 They (are / have got) tall.   ☐

2 They (are / have got) short hair.   ☐

5 Match the questions in Activity 3 with the pictures in Activity 4.

1 ☐ b   2 ☐   3 ☐

6 🎧 1:08 Listen and complete.

	Dad	Mum	Grandad
hair	bald		
eyes			
other			

7 Write sentences about the people in Activity 6 in your notebook.

📌 Dad's tall and bald. He's got...

8 Read and match.

1 She's got a lot of friends because
2 She's got a lot of friends but
3 She's got a lot of friends and
4 I'm tall because
5 I'm tall but
6 I'm tall and

a she hasn't got brothers or sisters.
b she's got a lot of pets.
c she's funny and kind.
d I've got straight black hair.
e my mum and dad are tall.
f I'm not two metres tall!

9 Complete the words.

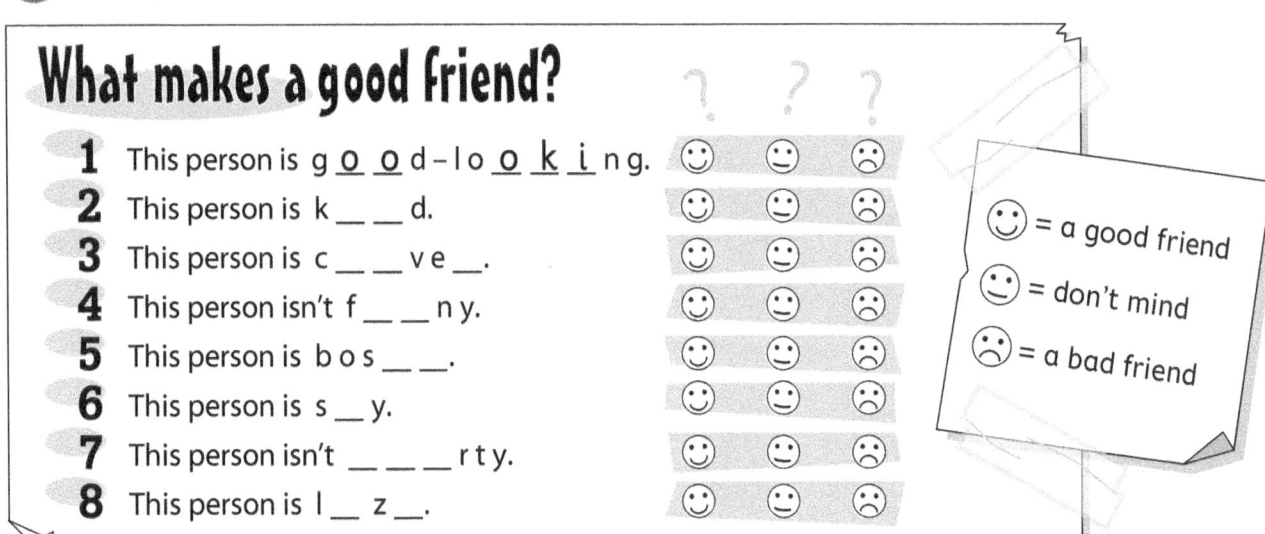

What makes a good friend?

1 This person is g o o d–lo o k i ng. ☺ ☺ ☹
2 This person is k __ __ d. ☺ ☺ ☹
3 This person is c __ __ ve __. ☺ ☺ ☹
4 This person isn't f __ __ n y. ☺ ☺ ☹
5 This person is b o s __ __. ☺ ☺ ☹
6 This person is s __ y. ☺ ☺ ☹
7 This person isn't __ __ __ r t y. ☺ ☺ ☹
8 This person is l __ z __. ☺ ☺ ☹

☺ = a good friend
☺ = don't mind
☹ = a bad friend

10 What makes a good friend? Read and choose in Activity 9.

11 Write about your good friend.

My Friend

Tell us about your friend!

_____ is _____ and _____.

He/She's _____ but I don't mind.

He/She's my friend because _____.

SUBMIT ▶

Lesson 3 🎧 **Sing.** (See Pupil's Book page 6.)

1:10
1:11

12 Say and complete. Then listen and check.

~~bossy~~ by cry fly granny lazy ~~my~~ spiky sporty ugly

shy
my
_____
_____
_____

funny
bossy
_____
_____
_____
_____
_____

13 Listen. Where is Carlos? Is he happy?

14 Listen again and match.

1 Megan is

2 The mum and dad are

3 The food is

a short.

b nice.

c funny.

d kind.

e bossy.

15 Imagine you are staying with this family in Britain. Look and write to a friend.

bad curly good time is bossy nice spiky straight

Emily   Steven

○○○ **Subject:** My stay in Britain!

Dear_____,

I'm having a ¹_____ here in Britain.

Emily is ²_____. She's got ³_____

hair. Steven has got ⁴_____ hair, and he is

⁵_____. Their mum ⁶_____.

She's got ⁷_____ hair.

Love,

_____

16 Write.

Hector Frost   Mike   Polly   ~~Smith~~

①    ②    ③   ④

__Smith__   _____   _____   _____

17 Look at the story and tick (✔).

1 Who are Mike and Polly following?

ⓐ    ⓑ    ⓒ

☐   ☐   ☐

2 What does Polly hear at 2.00 a.m.?

ⓐ 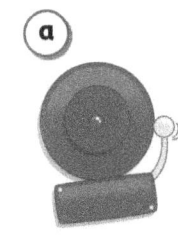   ⓑ    ⓒ

☐   ☐   ☐

18 Find the words in the story and write.

1 These two words mean 'Let's go'.   __Come on__

2 Hair growing on a man's face.   _____

3 People who steal.   _____

4 An idea for what to do next.   _____

5 A red fruit.   _____

6 To walk behind someone.   _____

19 Look, think and complete. Then add two more.

~~sun~~

cloud   lion   ~~water~~

frog   fire

warm colours	cool colours
sun	water
_____	_____
_____	_____
_____	_____

20 Look, listen and choose.

These pictures are by an artist called Dürer. The pictures are of the artist.

 **a**

 **b**

21 Find and write the questions. Then answer about Picture a.

does   he   he   ~~how~~   is   like   look   old   what

1   How _____ ?   He _____ .

2   _____   _____

22 **Read and write.**

Talking about appearance

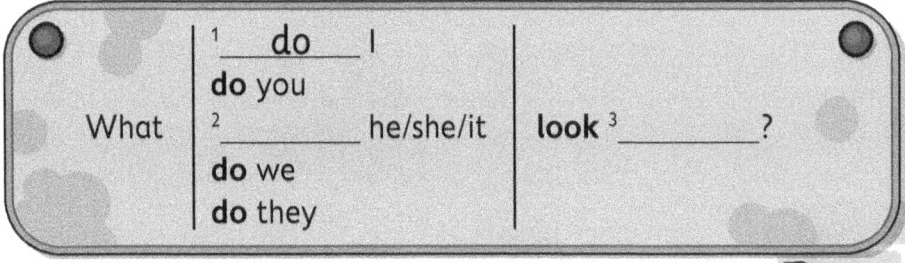

	¹ ___do___ I	
	do you	
What	² _____ he/she/it	**look** ³ _____ ?
	do we	
	do they	

I'm not very clever but I'm sporty and I'm good-looking.

I like you because you're funny!

23 **Write.**

bald   beautiful   blue eyes
cute   good-looking
long hair   spiky hair
straight hair

am/is/are	have/has got
bald	

24 **Write. Then number.**

1   What ___does___ she look like? _____ tall and has got spiky black hair.

2   What _____ he look like? _____ short and bald.

3   What _____ they look like? _____ beautiful and have got long straight hair.

a   **1**

b

c

25 Look at Activity 24 and write the answers.

> kind   lazy   sporty

1   (Picture a) She's _____.

2   (Picture b) They're _____.

3   (Picture c) He's _____.

26 Listen and write.

1:21

> bossy   clever   lazy   likes   ~~name~~   shy   spiky   sporty   tall

My friend

My friend's ¹_____name_____ is Miki. She's ²_____ and she's
got short ³_____ hair. She's got brown eyes and she wears
glasses. She ⁴_____ skirts and colourful T-shirts.

She isn't ⁵_____ or ⁶_____. She's a bit
⁷_____ but it's OK. I like her because she's funny,
⁸_____ and ⁹_____.

27 Describe a friend or family member. Use *He's/She's* and *He's/She's got...*

What does he/she look like? _____

_____

_____

What's he/she like? _____

_____

_____

_____

⭐ **Are you ready for Unit 2?**

2 My life

1 Read and match.

1	be	g	**2**	take		**3**	make		**4**	tidy
5	brush		**6**	meet		**7**	do		**8**	wash

a my homework   **c** my room   **e** my friends   **g** on time

b notes in class   **d** my face   **f** my bed   **h** my teeth

2 Look and write. Then listen and tick (✓) or cross (✗) for Dan.

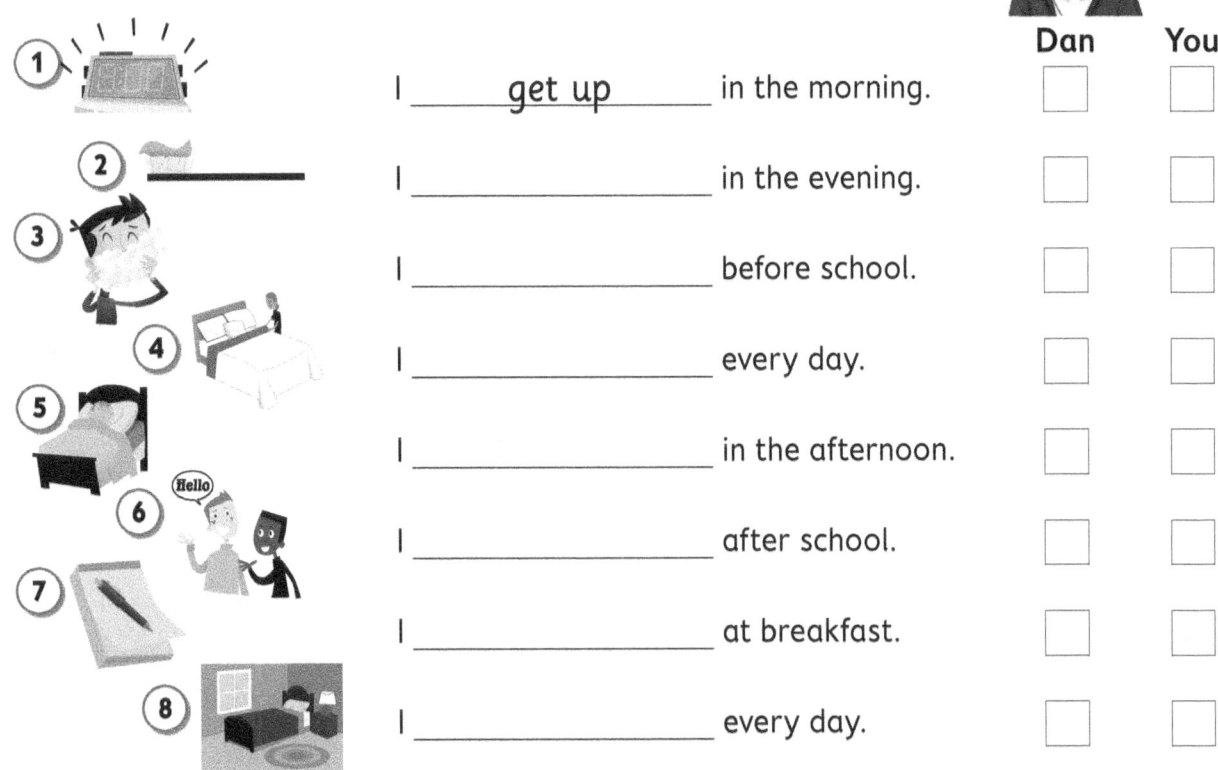

	Dan	You
1 I ___get up___ in the morning.	☐	☐
2 I _____ in the evening.	☐	☐
3 I _____ before school.	☐	☐
4 I _____ every day.	☐	☐
5 I _____ in the afternoon.	☐	☐
6 I _____ after school.	☐	☐
7 I _____ at breakfast.	☐	☐
8 I _____ every day.	☐	☐

3 Tick (✓) or cross (✗) the sentences for you.

4 Correct the sentences with a cross (✗) in your notebook.

> I don't get up in the afternoon. I get up in the morning.

5 Find and circle seven words. Then write.

y o u r h i s t h e i r t s y h e r o u r m y

1	I	→	_____
2	you	→	_____your_____
3	he	→	_____
4	she	→	_____
5	it	→	_____
6	we	→	_____
7	they	→	_____

6 Read and choose.

At half past eight every day, Dan and ¹(their / (his)) friend, Maddy, go to school by bus. But today there's a problem. It's nine o'clock and ²(their / its) bus isn't here!

Dan: Let's go to school by bike.

Maddy: I can't ride ³(her / my) bike. It's only got one of ⁴(his / its) wheels.

Dan: My sister's got a bike. Ride that!

Maddy: But ⁵(your / her) sister is eighteen. ⁶(Their / Her) bike is very big.

Dan: Look! It's OK. ⁷(Our / His) bus is here now!

7  What do they do on Saturdays? Listen and match.

1	Robbie and Emma		**a**	do/homework
2	Their mum and dad		**b**	tidy/room
3	Maddy		**c**	read/books in bed
4	Dan		**d**	play/favourite computer games

8  Listen again. Write sentences in your notebook.

1 Robbie and Emma don't tidy their rooms on Saturdays. They play their favourite computer games.

2 Their mum and dad...

9 **Look and write.**

always   never   ~~never~~   often   sometimes   usually

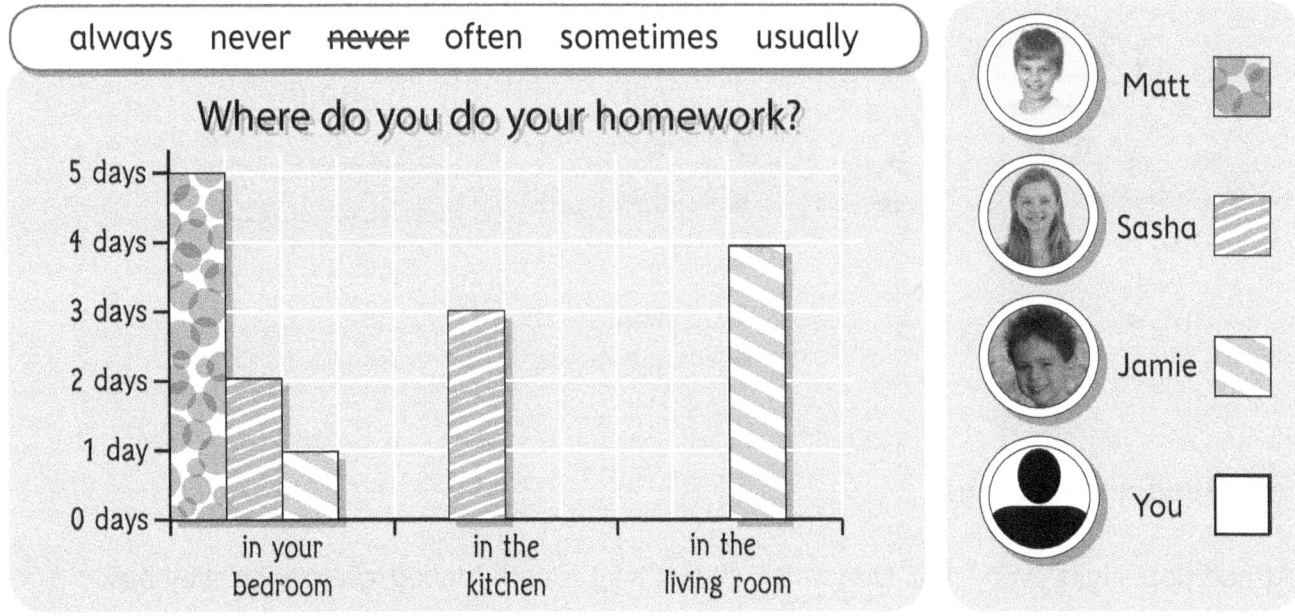

Where do you do your homework?

	Matt	
	Sasha	
	Jamie	
	You	

1 Matt _____never_____ does his homework in the kitchen.

2 Sasha _____ does her homework in the kitchen.

3 Matt _____ does his homework in his bedroom.

4 Sasha and Matt _____ do their homework in the living room.

5 Sasha _____ does her homework in her bedroom.

6 Jamie _____ does his homework in the living room.

10 **Complete the chart for you. Write sentences in your notebook.**

I usually do my homework in my bedroom.

11 **Find and write.**

····· the dog

····· Matt

····· Jamie

····· Sasha

1 This is _____Jamie's_____ skateboard.

2 This is _____ ball.

3 This is _____ brother.

4 This is _____ bike.

12 Write the correct form of the words in brackets.

a He ____goes____ (go) to school.

b She _____ (watch) TV.

c He _____ (make) his bed.

d She _____ (wash) her face.

e She _____ (do) her homework.

f He _____ (brush) his hair.

13  Count and write the number of syllables in the new words. Listen, check and say.

a [1]   **b** [ ]   **c** [ ]   **d** [ ]   **e** [ ]   **f** [ ]

14 Listen and write.

I don't like mornings. My big brother
¹____always____ gets up at five o'clock because
he's a farmer. He washes his face and makes
his breakfast. He ²_____ sings songs
in the morning. ³_____ songs are
horrible. I can't sleep after that.
I ⁴_____ get up at six o'clock because
I'm hungry. I like eggs for breakfast but I
⁵_____ eat toast. Why? Because my
brother eats ⁶_____ eggs at half past
five. Grrr!

15 Complete for you.

My Saturday morning

Time	Activity
	get up
	have breakfast

16 Write about your Saturday morning in your notebook.

On Saturday morning,
I usually get up at nine
o'clock. I...

17 **Look at the story and write.**

1   Polly and Mike watch _____Smith_____ keeping fit at the training camp.

2   They hide inside an _____.

3   They make a _____ to keep warm.

4   But then they go to _____!

5   Smith leaves his _____ at the training camp.

6   The red ribbons are the same as the ribbons in the _____.

18 **Look and write.**

> eats dinner ~~eats lunch~~ goes to bed
> tidies his room   washes the dog   watches TV

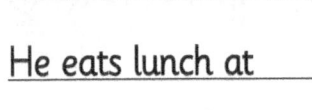

He eats lunch at

half past twelve.

_____   _____

_____   _____

_____   _____   _____

_____   _____   _____

19 **Read and circle.** *True* (✓) or *false* (X)? **Then find and write the answer.**

Health Quiz

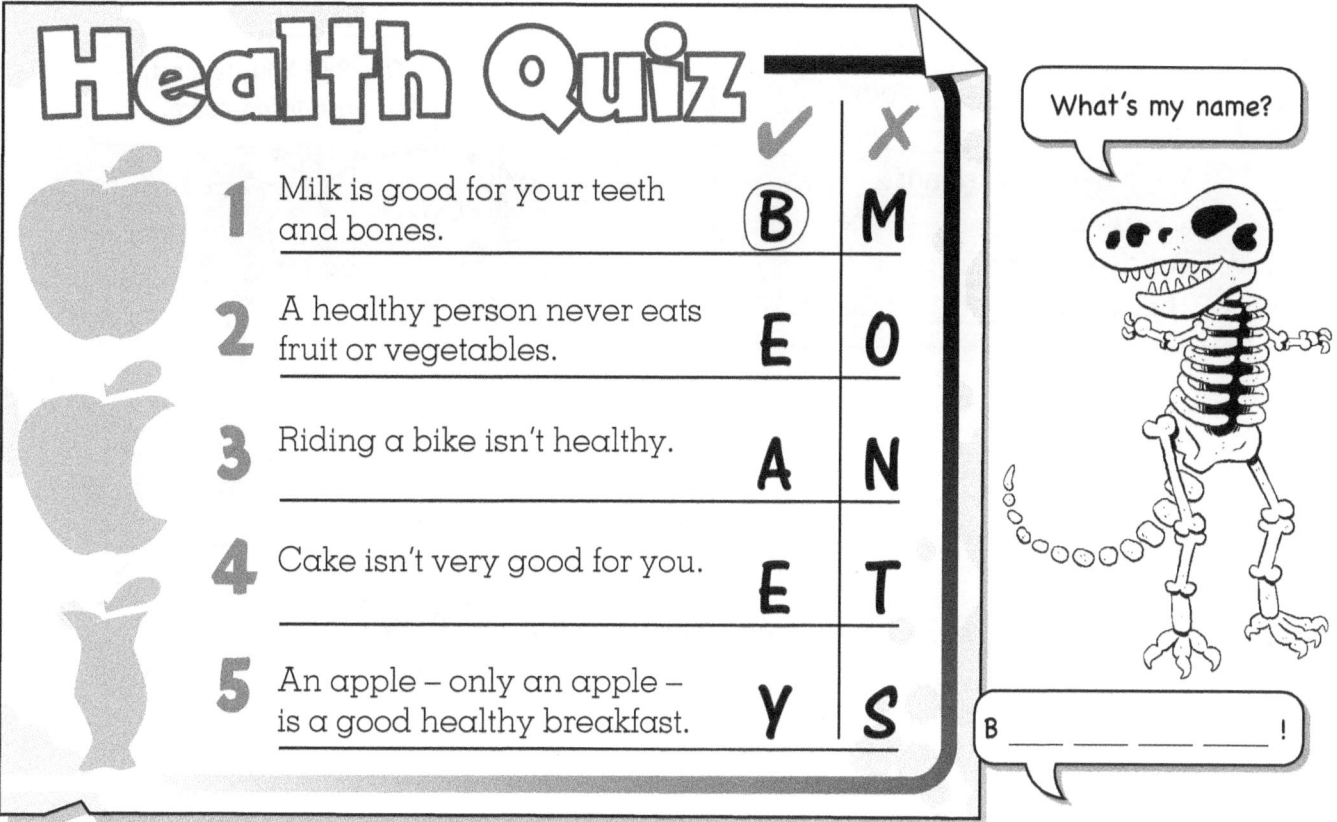

		✓	X
1	Milk is good for your teeth and bones.	(B)	M
2	A healthy person never eats fruit or vegetables.	E	O
3	Riding a bike isn't healthy.	A	N
4	Cake isn't very good for you.	E	T
5	An apple – only an apple – is a good healthy breakfast.	Y	S

What's my name?

B _ _ _ _ _ !

20 **Listen, read and find five differences. Listen again and correct.**

Application form

MUDCHESTER UNITED

We want healthy football players for Mudchester United. Write about your day.

           ten
I get up at ~~seven~~ o'clock. I have eggs on toast for breakfast.

I always brush my teeth after breakfast. I often play football

after dinner. After that, I wash my face and I go to bed at

nine o'clock.

21 Read and write.

Possessive adjectives

I brush **my** hair.
You tidy [1] __your__ room.
He makes [2] _____ bed.
She meets **her** friends.
It washes [3] _____ face.
We do **our** homework.
They brush [4] _____ teeth.

Oh, Bill! You never tidy the living room.

Sorry, Mum!

22 Read and choose.

Lucy and Lily are [1](sister's /(sisters)).
Lucy often does [2](his / her) homework in
[3](Lily /Lily's) bedroom because Lily has
got a computer. In the afternoon, they
meet [4](they / their) friends at the park.
Lucy has got a skateboard. [5](Lily / Lucy)
sometimes goes on [6](Lily's / Lucy's)
skateboard. Watch out, Lily!

23 Read again and write. *True* or *false*?

1 Lucy has got a computer. __False__

2 Lucy often does her homework on the computer. _____

3 They meet their friends in the morning. _____

4 Lily always goes on Lucy's skateboard. _____

24 **Read and write. Then listen and check.**

always   dinner   ~~do~~   help   usually   wash

My evenings

In the evening, I ¹_____do_____ my homework. I ²_____
do my homework before ³_____. After dinner, I ⁴_____
my mum tidy the kitchen and ⁵_____ the dishes. I ⁶_____ go
to bed at ten but sometimes I'm late.

25 **Describe a friend or family member.**

In the morning, _____. After breakfast, _____
_____. In the afternoon, _____. In
the evening, _____ before dinner. _____
to bed at _____. _____
_____
_____
_____
_____
_____
_____
_____
_____
_____
_____
_____
_____

 Are you ready for Unit 3?

3 Free time

1 Complete the words and match. Then draw the missing picture.

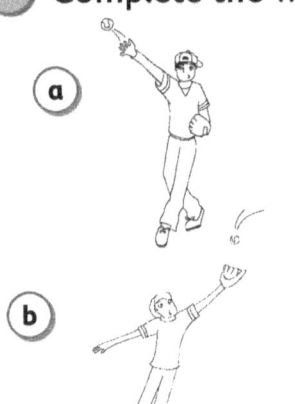

(a)

(b)

(c)

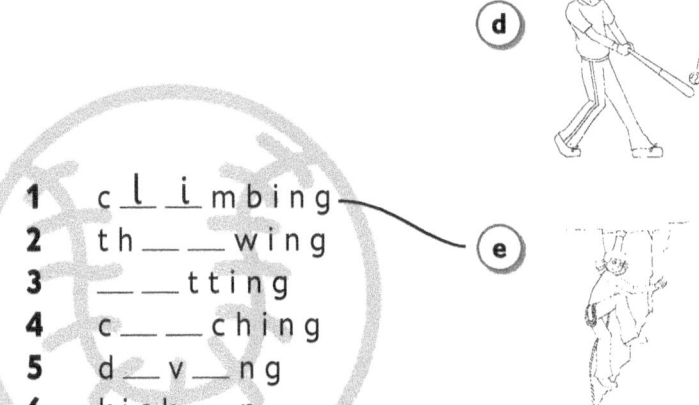

1 c l i m b i n g
2 t h __ __ w i n g
3 __ __ t t i n g
4 c __ __ c h i n g
5 d __ v __ n g
6 k i c k __ n __

(d)

(e)

(f)

2 Look and write.

Robbie

Dan

1 I'm good at _____throwing_____.

2 I'm not good at _____.

3 I'm good at _____.

4 I'm good at _____.

5 I'm not good at _____.

6 I'm good at _____.

3  Listen and say who is talking.

4 Look and write. Then listen and check.

am   are   at   good   ~~I'm~~   isn't   they're

Yes, I [6]_____ but [7]_____ good at jumping!

1
[1] I'm good
[2]_____ throwing.

He [3]_____ good at catching.

2

3
[4]_____ you
[5]_____ at climbing?

4

---

5 Look and write questions. Then ask a friend and choose.

1 Are you good at kicking? _____   (Yes, I am. / No, I'm not.)

2 _____   (Yes, I am. / No, I'm not.)

3 _____   (Yes, I am. / No, I'm not.)

4 _____   (Yes, I am. / No, I'm not.)

5 _____   (Yes, I am. / No, I'm not.)

6 _____   (Yes, I am. / No, I'm not.)

7 _____   (Yes, I am. / No, I'm not.)

6 Write about your friend in your notebook.

> Charlie is good at kicking and sailing but he isn't good at climbing and diving.

7 Complete the crossword. Then find and write.

I love S __ __ __ __ __ __ __ __ !

1 | s | k | a | t | e | b | o | a | r | d | i | n | g |

2 | | | l | | | | | | | | |

3 | | | | y | | | |

5

4 | | | | | s

5 | t | | | | |

6 | | c |

7 | | a | |

8 Look and write.

1 He loves trampolining.

2 _____

3 _____

4 _____

5 _____

6 _____

🏆 = is/are good at

♡ = loves/love

😠 = doesn't/ don't like

9 Find and write. Then listen and answer for Robbie.

1 (like) (you) (do) (doing) (~~what~~)   2 (at) (you) (good) (are) (what)

What _____ ?   _____

I _____ .   _____

10 **Read. Is Ellie good at doing sport?**

Dear Granny,
Action Camp is great! I'm here with Ellie because we both love doing sports. We go swimming every morning. I love swimming. I can swim 15 metres underwater now. We have diving lessons, too. I'm not very good at diving because I feel scared but Ellie can dive from the big diving board. She's fantastic! Ellie and I like trampolining after lunch and we love playing tennis together in the afternoon. Ellie's very good at running and hitting the ball.
Lots of love,
Mark

11 **Read and answer.**

1 What does Mark do in the morning?   Mark goes swimming in the morning.

2 Can Mark swim?   _____

3 Is Mark good at diving?   _____

4 Is Ellie good at diving?   _____

5 What do they like doing after lunch?   _____

6 Do they like playing tennis?   _____

12 **Look and complete. Write the -ing forms.**

dance dive fish hit kick paint ride run swim

+ ing		+ last letter + ing		- e + ing	
kick	kicking	swim	swimming	dance	dancing
_____	_____	_____	_____	_____	_____
_____	_____	_____	_____	_____	_____

13 **Imagine you're at a camp. Write a letter to a friend in your notebook.**

Dear Lucy,
I'm at Beach Camp this week. I love...

14 **Look at the story and circle. *True* or *False*?**
Correct the false sentences.

1 Polly can hear the skidoo.

(True)/ False _____

2 Mike's mum makes them breakfast.

True / False _____

3 Polly finds another ribbon outside.

True / False _____

4 Mike always plays football on Sundays.

True / False _____

5 They see wolf tracks.

True / False _____

15 **Read and write.**

①

Are they good at __running races__?

Yes, they are.

②

Is he good at diving?

_____

③

Does he love _____?

_____

④

_____

No, they aren't.

16 Read and write. Then listen and check.

good at ~~my~~ play playing
sometimes write writing

Hi. ¹____My____ name's David. I have guitar lessons every week. I love ²_____ the guitar – my teacher is great. My friend, Melissa, is ³_____ singing and her brother can ⁴_____ the drums. We ⁵_____ play songs together. It's fun! I like ⁶_____ music, too. One day, I want to ⁷_____ music for films.

17 Listen to the music and tick (✓) for you.

1	cool	☐	OK	☐	bad	☐	**2**	cool	☐	OK	☐	bad	☐
3	cool	☐	OK	☐	bad	☐	**4**	cool	☐	OK	☐	bad	☐
5	cool	☐	OK	☐	bad	☐	**6**	cool	☐	OK	☐	bad	☐
7	cool	☐	OK	☐	bad	☐	**8**	cool	☐	OK	☐	bad	☐

18 Listen again and choose your favourite. Then find that number and read about you.

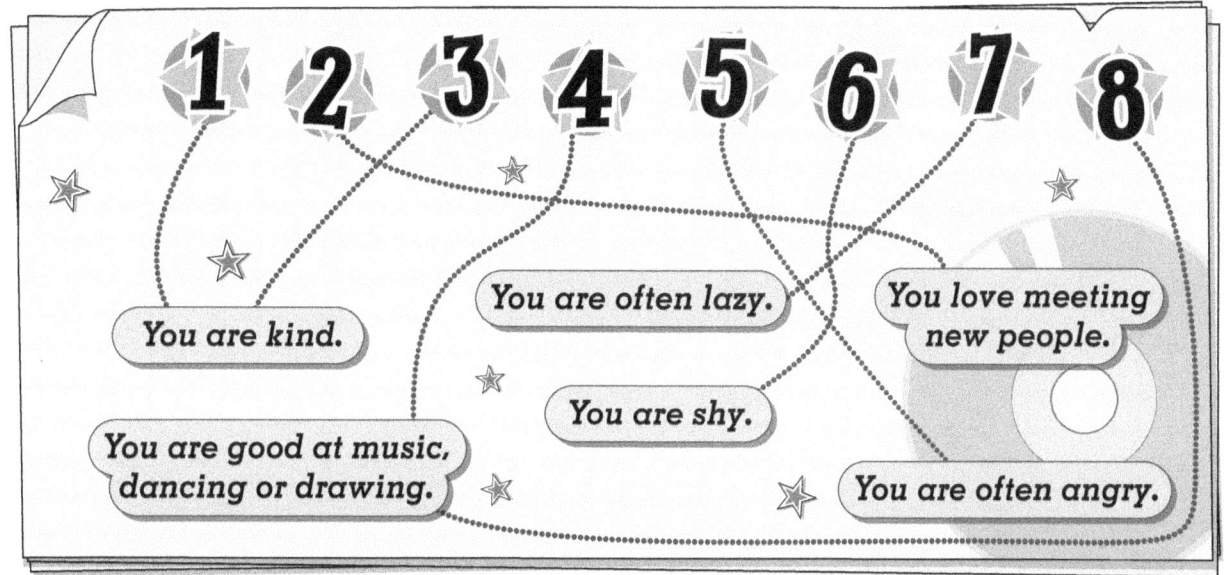

1 2 3 4 5 6 7 8

You are kind.

You are often lazy.

You love meeting new people.

You are good at music, dancing or drawing.

You are shy.

You are often angry.

Talking about abilities

I'm/I'm not You [1]**'re** /You **aren't** He**'s**/He **isn't** She**'s**/She **isn't** It**'s**/It **isn't** We**'re**/We [2]_____ They**'re**/They **aren't**	**good at**	sing**ing**.

I love singing!

But he isn't good at singing!

What do you **like** doing?	I **like** acting and I **love** diving.
What [3]_____ you **good at**?	I'm **good at** hitting a ball.

20  **Look and write. Then listen and choose.**
True or false?

	= is/are good at
	= loves/love
✔	= can
✗	= can't
	= doesn't/don't like

1 Sam

Sam loves playing the guitar.   (True)/ False

2 Anna ✗  _____ True / False

3 The children  _____ True / False

4 Rick  _____ True / False

5 Jo and Flo ✔ _____ True / False

6 Bill  _____ True / False

21   **Read and write. Then listen and check.**

but   go   good   love   not   ~~playing~~   play   usually

My activities

I like ¹ __playing__ tennis. I play tennis at a club. I ² _____ play in
the afternoon. We ³ _____ games on Sundays. I love swimming, too.
I ⁴ _____ swimming on Monday and Thursday. I ⁵ _____ swimming
in the sea in the summer, too. At school, I'm ⁶ _____ at sports and English.
I'm ⁷ _____ good at Art ⁸ _____ the teacher helps me a lot.

22 **Write about things you like, don't like and things you can do.**

I love _____ and _____ but I don't

like _____ or _____ . I'm good

at _____ and _____ but I'm not

good at _____ or _____ .

_____

_____

_____

_____

_____

_____

_____

_____

_____

 Are you ready for Unit 4?

1 Complete the words.

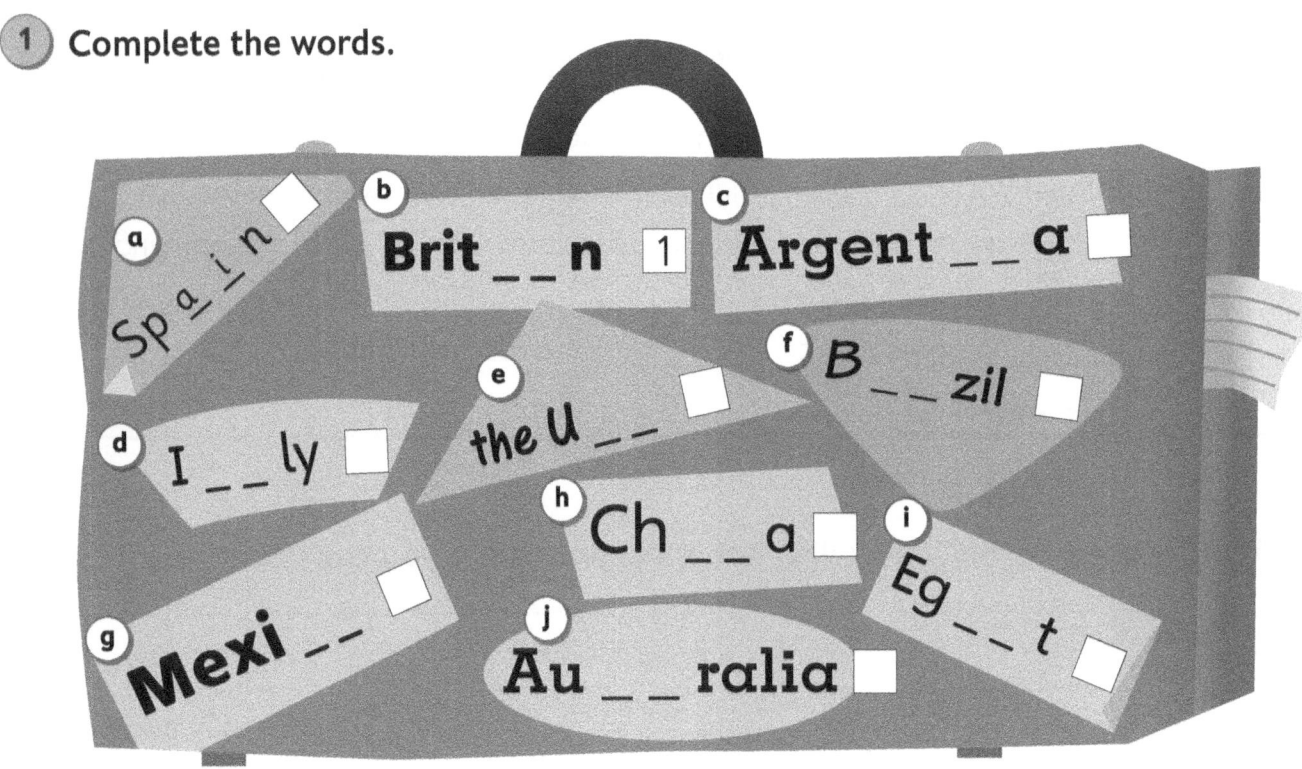

a Sp a i n ☐

b Brit _ _ n 1

c Argent _ _ a ☐

d I _ _ ly ☐

e the U _ _ ☐

f B _ _ zil ☐

g Mexi _ _ ☐

h Ch _ _ a ☐

i Eg _ _ t ☐

j Au _ _ ralia ☐

2 Listen and number the countries in order.

3 Complete the crossword with words from Activity 1.

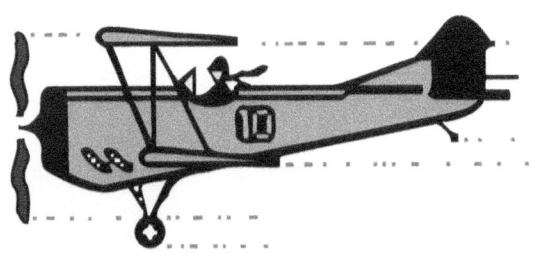

4 **Listen and draw.**

5 **Read and write *a*, *some* or *any*.**

1 There are ___some___ long rivers in the USA.

2 There isn't _____ rainforest in Italy.

3 There aren't _____ giraffes in Britain.

4 There are _____ old houses in Spain.

5 There's _____ big waterfall in Brazil and Argentina.

6 **Look and write.**

1 hippos/China ✗

There aren't any hippos in China.

2 a rainforest/Australia ✓

_____

3 a snowy mountain/Egypt ✗

_____

4 elephants/Mexico ✗

_____

5 beautiful beaches/Spain ✓

_____

7 **Write about your country in your notebook.**

There are some pretty beaches in my country.

8 Find and circle eight words. Then find and write the answer using the letters that aren't circled.

SONG

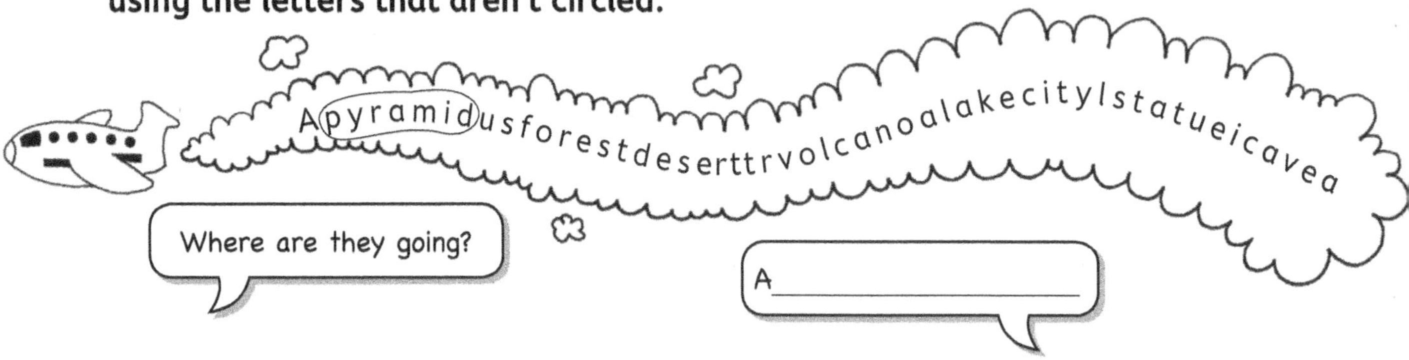

A p y r a m i d u s f o r e s t d e s e r t t r v o l c a n o a l a k e c i t y l s t a t u e i c a v e a

Where are they going?

A_____

9 Look and complete. Use words from Activity 8.

			Britain	Spain
1		lakes	✓	✓
2	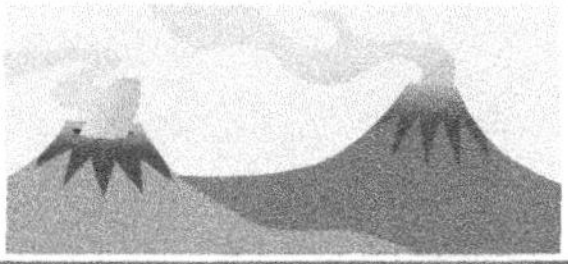	_____es	✗	✓
3		a big _____	✓	✓
4		_____s	✓	✓
5	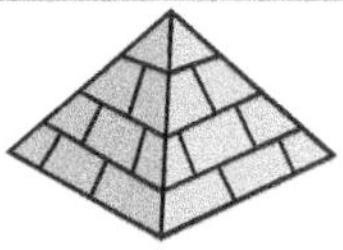	a big _____	✗	✗
6		_____s	✓	✓
7		a _____	✗	✓
8		a _____	✓	✓

10 Look at Activity 9. Write questions and answers in your notebook.

1 Are there any lakes in Britain? Yes, there are.

11  **Read and write *ear*, *air* or *ere*. Then listen and say.**

¹Wh**ere**_____ is Claire?
She's ²th_____, on the ³ch_____.
She's ⁴w_____ing a dress and a
⁵b_____ in her ⁶h_____.

12  **Listen. Which country is Mia in now?**

13  **Listen again and choose.**

1 Mia is talking to her (grandad /(granny)).

2 She's in a (rainforest / city).

3 There are some (beaches / pyramids) in Rio.

4 There's a big (island / statue), too.

5 Brazilian people are good at (dancing / singing).

14  **Read and write. Then listen and check.**

animals beautiful ~~Grandad~~ lake trees rainforest

Dear ¹Grandad,
Hello from the Amazon ²_____
in Brazil! There are a lot of tall green
³_____ in the rainforest and some
dangerous ⁴_____ , too! I'm fishing
in a ⁵_____ today. I can see some
monkeys! It's very ⁶_____ here.
Lots of love,
Mia

POSTAL SYSTEM EGYPT
SEP 12
GIZA

Mr Tracy
15 Warwick Close
Upton, PV17 3BP
Britain

15 **Think about your favourite holiday. Write a postcard in your notebook.**

Dear Matt,
I'm having a great time here in the USA. There are...

16 **Read and correct.**

1   Hector Frost has got a map.

<u>Polly has got a map</u>.

2   There aren't any roads to the pyramid.

_____

3   There are some tracks going south.

_____

4   There aren't any ribbons on the dog.

_____

5   Frost is happy to see the children in the forest.

_____

17   **Listen and circle the correct dog.**

18   **Imagine. What happens next in the story?**

I think <u>the Ice Detectives are going to Bollington Hall and</u> _____

_____

_____.

Come to Greenland!

1 ___Ride___ on skidoos!

Climb snowy 2_____!

See 3_____ and waterfalls of ice!

There aren't 4_____ big cities here but there

are 5_____ beautiful polar 6_____ and

reindeer in this cold place. Every 7_____ in

Greenland is an adventure!

Greenland – a world of ❄ice!

20 **Read and choose.**

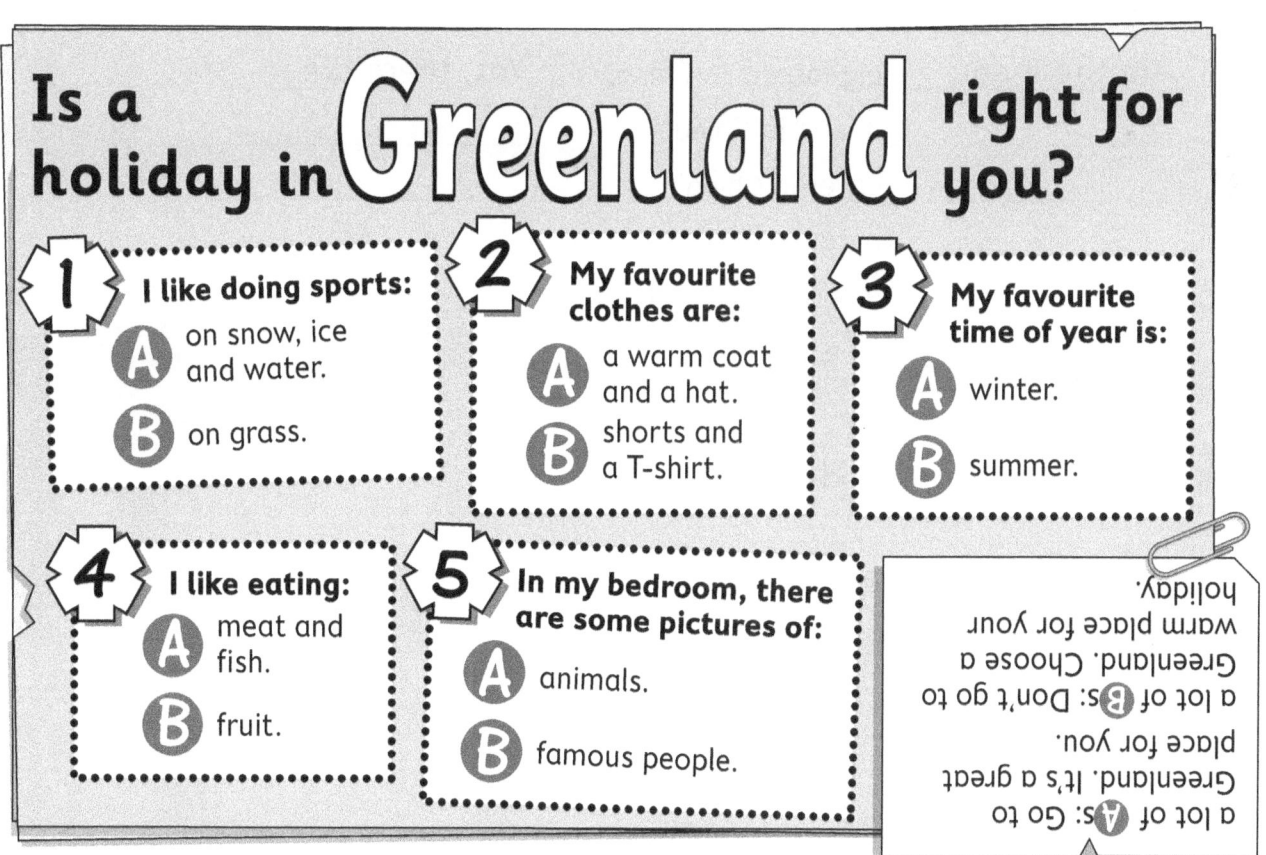

Is a holiday in Greenland right for you?

1 **I like doing sports:**
- Ⓐ on snow, ice and water.
- Ⓑ on grass.

2 **My favourite clothes are:**
- Ⓐ a warm coat and a hat.
- Ⓑ shorts and a T-shirt.

3 **My favourite time of year is:**
- Ⓐ winter.
- Ⓑ summer.

4 **I like eating:**
- Ⓐ meat and fish.
- Ⓑ fruit.

5 **In my bedroom, there are some pictures of:**
- Ⓐ animals.
- Ⓑ famous people.

a lot of Ⓐs: Go to Greenland. It's a great place for you.
a lot of Ⓑs: Don't go to Greenland. Choose a warm place for your holiday.

21 **Read and write.**

a, some and *any*

There's ¹ ___a___ lake.
There **isn't** ² _____ forest.
There **are** ³ _____ cities.
There **aren't** ⁴ _____ statues.

Is there ⁵ _____ statue?	Yes, there **is**. No, there **isn't**.
Are there ⁶ _____ caves?	Yes, there **are**. No, there **aren't**.

Are there any pyramids?

Yes, there are!

---

22 **Read and write the questions. Then listen and write the answers.**

1	<u>Are there any</u>	big forests in China?	<u>Yes, there are.</u>
2	_____	desert in China?	_____
3	_____	caves in China?	_____
4	_____	pyramids in China?	_____
5	_____	nice statues in China?	_____
6	_____	lions in China?	_____

23 **Listen again and choose.**

1 The boy ((wants) / doesn't want) to go to China.

2 The desert is called the (Gobi / Moby) Desert.

3 In China, some people (live / work) in caves.

4 The pyramids of China (are / aren't) famous.

5 There are statues of (horses / camels).

24   **Read and write. Then listen and check.**

> any   are   birds   fish   ~~on~~   sing
> sometimes   There   There's   under

The river

There's a river near my house. I go there ¹_____on_____ my bike.
² _____ aren't ³ _____ people near the river.
There ⁴ _____ a lot of trees and ⁵ _____ . The birds
⁶ _____ in the trees. There are ⁷ _____ in the river and
⁸ _____ they jump. ⁹ _____ a bridge over the river.
Sometimes, I sit ¹⁰ _____ the bridge and read. I love the river.

25 **Write about a place you know.**

There's a _____ and a _____ .

There isn't a _____ or a _____ .

There are some _____ .

There aren't any _____ .

_____

_____

_____

_____

_____

_____

_____

_____

 Are you ready for Unit 5?

5 Shopping

1 Find and circle.

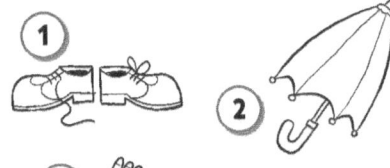

x	p	s	t	l	w	k	a	s	u
b	c	u	e	f	a	g	h	w	m
s	a	n	d	a	l	s	t	i	b
i	j	g	k	m	l	n	r	m	r
o	g	l	o	v	e	s	a	s	e
s	c	a	r	f	t	o	i	u	l
p	q	s	u	v	w	c	n	i	l
x	y	s	j	a	c	k	e	t	a
d	r	e	s	s	y	s	r	u	t
m	e	s	h	o	e	s	s	n	a

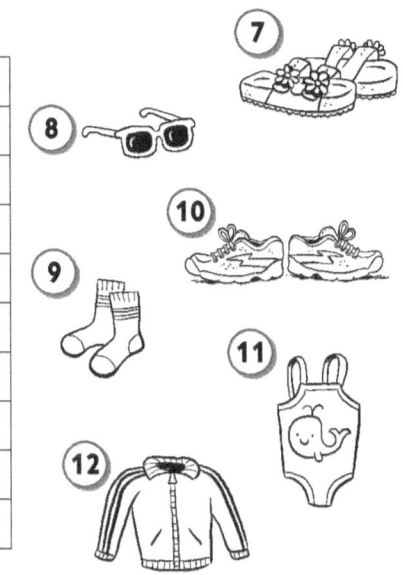

2 Look and write. Use *is/are* and words from Activity 1.

1 How much ____is____
that ____swimsuit____?

2 How much _____
those _____?

3 How much _____
that _____?

4 How much _____
those _____?

3 🎧 Listen. What does Maddy buy?

4 Look and write the prices in words.

1 _____ one thousand pounds _____
2 _____
3 _____
4 _____
5 _____
6 _____

5  The prices in Activity 4 are wrong. Listen and choose.

1   **a** £990   **b** £999   **c** £919   2   **a** £12.50   **b** £20.50   **c** £15.20

3   **a** £9.50   **b** £19.50   **c** £90.50   4   **a** £12   **b** £20   **c** £21

5   **a** £40.20   **b** £42.20   **c** £42   6   **a** £26.50   **b** £25.50   **c** £25.55

6  Read and write. Then listen and check.

course   how   hundred   ~~much~~   please   pounds

David: Hello. How ¹_____ much _____ is this umbrella, please?

Shop assistant: It's fourteen ²_____ fifty.

David: And ³_____ much are those shorts?

Shop assistant: They're one ⁴_____ pounds.

David: Oh... can I buy this umbrella, ⁵_____?

Shop assistant: Yes, of ⁶_____.

7 **Complete the words and match.**

1 c h _e_ _a_ p sunglasses [b]
2 d __ __ k grey socks [ ]
3 a l __ __ h t grey T-shirt [ ]
4 e x __ __ __ __ s __ v __ sunglasses [ ]
5 b __ g g __ jeans [ ]
6 a t __ g __ t jumper [ ]

8 **Look and write.**

baggy   dark   expensive   ~~tight~~

1

They're too tight.

2

It's _____

I can't see!

3

_____

4

_____

9 **Write about your clothes in your notebook. Use _too_.**

baggy   big   dark   light   long
old   short   small   tight

My green jumper is too tight.

10 Look and write *ight* or *ite*. Then listen and say.

My new ¹k__ite__ isn't dark. It's ²l_____.

The Moon is ³wh_____ at ⁴n_____.

The ⁵firef_____er's jacket is too ⁶t_____.

Do you use your ⁷r_____ hand when you ⁸wr_____?

11 Listen and tick (✓) the adverts the boys talk about.

¹ **BIKE,** blue, for a boy 160 cm tall, £123. Tel: 08459 2652741 ✓

² **COMPUTER GAMES,** twenty children's games, £17. gamer@yoho.it.uk ☐

³ **SCARF,** £6.50, red and white. footballfan@ bkinternet.co.uk ☐

⁴ **SKATEBOARD,** new, £38. Tel: 08459 4839223 ☐

⁵ **DOG,** six years old, black, good with children, wants a new home. Tel: 08459 3221345 ☐

⁶ **JACKET,** £25, white, for a four-year-old girl. whiteshop@intweb.com ☐

12 Listen again and write.

1 The bike in the advert is too ____big____.

2 The skateboard is too _____.

3 Tom's mum doesn't like _____.

4 Tom wants to buy the _____.

13 Write three adverts. Then look at your friend's adverts and talk about them.

I want a toy robot but £20 is too expensive.

14 **Look at the story and write.**

1   Who is helping the explorers in the shop? <u>Polly's mum.</u>

2   What costs 500 Ice pounds? _____

3   Who wants to go to the lake? _____

4   Who is hiding near the lake? _____

5   Who does Smith push into the lake? _____

6   Does Gizmo catch Smith? _____

15   **Listen and write the prices. What does the Queen buy?**

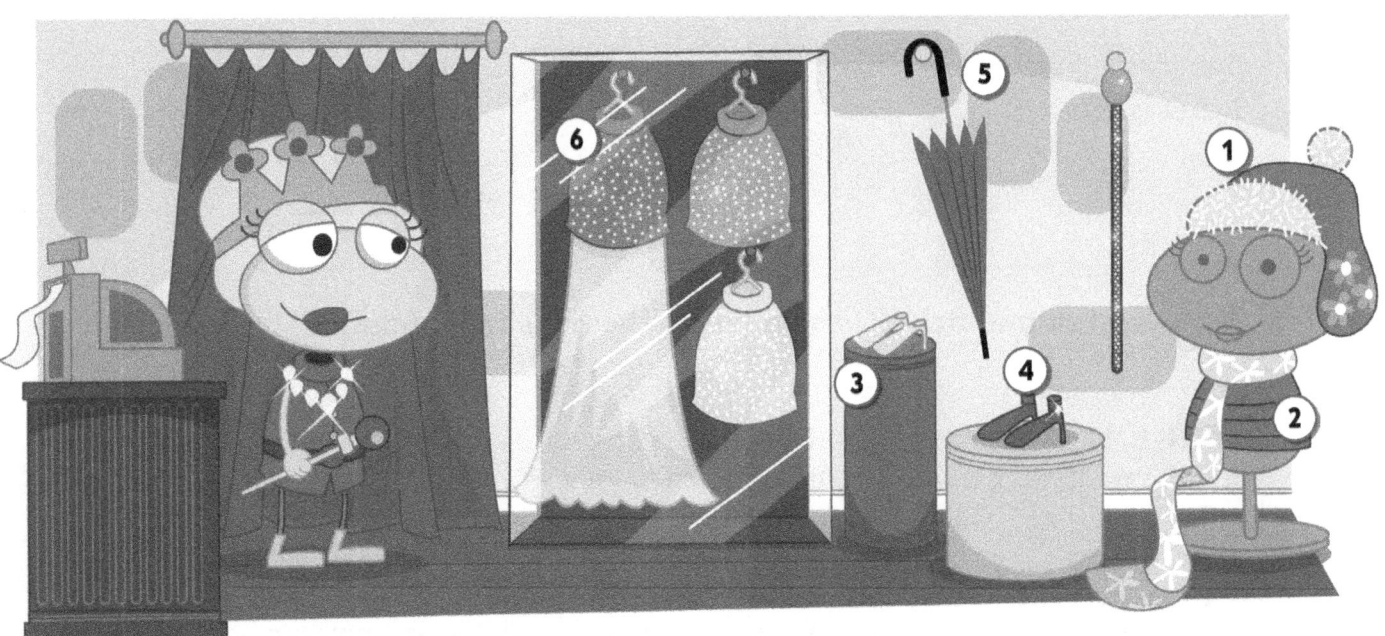

1   <u>£9.99</u>   2   _____   3   _____

4   _____   5   _____   6   _____

16 **Imagine. What happens next in the story?**

I think _____

_____ .

17 **Read and write.**

| A swimsuit   A warm jacket   Sailing shoes   Sunglasses   ~~Trousers and a T-shirt~~ |

Winderton Sailing School

Clothes list for sailing lessons

1   Trousers and a T-shirt
*Don't wear your favourite clothes. Choose
something old and not too expensive.*

2   _____
*At sea, it's often too windy for summer clothes,
even on sunny days.*

3   _____
*The sunlight on the water is very bad for your
eyes.*

4   _____
Our boats are too wet for trainers or sandals.

5   _____
*After the lessons, you can dive from the boat
and have fun in the water.*

18  **Listen and complete.**

	Activity	Clothes
	1 sailing	2 warm _____ 3 _____ 4 _____
	5 _____	6 _____ 7 _____ 8 _____ trousers
	9 _____	10 long _____ 11 _____ 12 _____

19 **Think of an activity and make a list.
Your friend guesses the activity.**

I've got a swimsuit...

20 Read and write.

I love this hat but it's too small.

And this hat is too big...

Talking about prices

How ¹ <u>much</u> **is** that jacket?	**It's** one thousand pounds!
How much ² _____ those gloves?	**They're** four pounds fifty.
Can I ³ _____ this swimsuit, please?	Yes, of course. Five pounds, please.

too + adjective

It's They're	⁴ _____	expensive.

21 Order the sentences to make a dialogue. Then listen and check.

2:49

a **Nina:** Oh! It's too expensive. I've only got twenty pounds. How much are those dark blue jeans? ☐

b **Shop assistant:** Yes, of course. Eight pounds, please. ☐

c **Nina:** Great. Can I buy it, please? ☐

d **Shop assistant:** They're eighteen pounds fifty. ☐

e **Nina:** Well, they're cheap but they're too baggy. I like wearing tight jeans. How much is that scarf? ☐

f **Shop assistant:** The jumper's twenty-one pounds. ☐

g **Nina:** Excuse me. How much is that jumper? 1

h **Shop assistant:** It's eight pounds. ☐

22 Listen again and tick (✓) the true sentences.

1 The jumper is too expensive. ✓

2 Nina has got twenty-one pounds. ☐

3 The jeans are dark blue and tight. ☐

4 The jeans are dark blue, baggy and cheap. ☐

5 The scarf is eighteen pounds fifty. ☐

6 Nina buys the scarf. ☐

23 Read and write. Then listen and check.

> back   because   colours   red   sandals
> tight   too   ~~T-shirt~~   trainers

My clothes

My favourite ¹_____T-shirt_____ is white with small letters on the

²_____. It's really cool. My favourite shoes are my

³_____. They're ⁴_____ and black. I don't like my

winter boots ⁵_____ they're too ⁶_____ and my

summer ⁷_____ are ⁸_____ small now. I really like my

jacket. It's green and yellow. They're my favourite ⁹_____.

24 Write about your clothes. Use: *My favourite... is/are...; It/They...;*
I don't like my... because it's/they're too...

_____

_____

_____

_____

_____

 Are you ready for Unit 6?

Lesson 8   43

6 Party time

1 **Complete the words. Then look and write the names.**

1 Martin and Becky are my p _a_ _r_ _e_ n t s.

2 Saskia and her brother, Ollie, are my c __ __ s __ n s.

3 Caroline is my a __ __ t.

4 Andy is my u __ c l __.

5 Sue is my gra __ n __.

6 Sue and John are my g r __ __ d p __ __ e n t s.

> Hi, I'm Dan and this is my family.

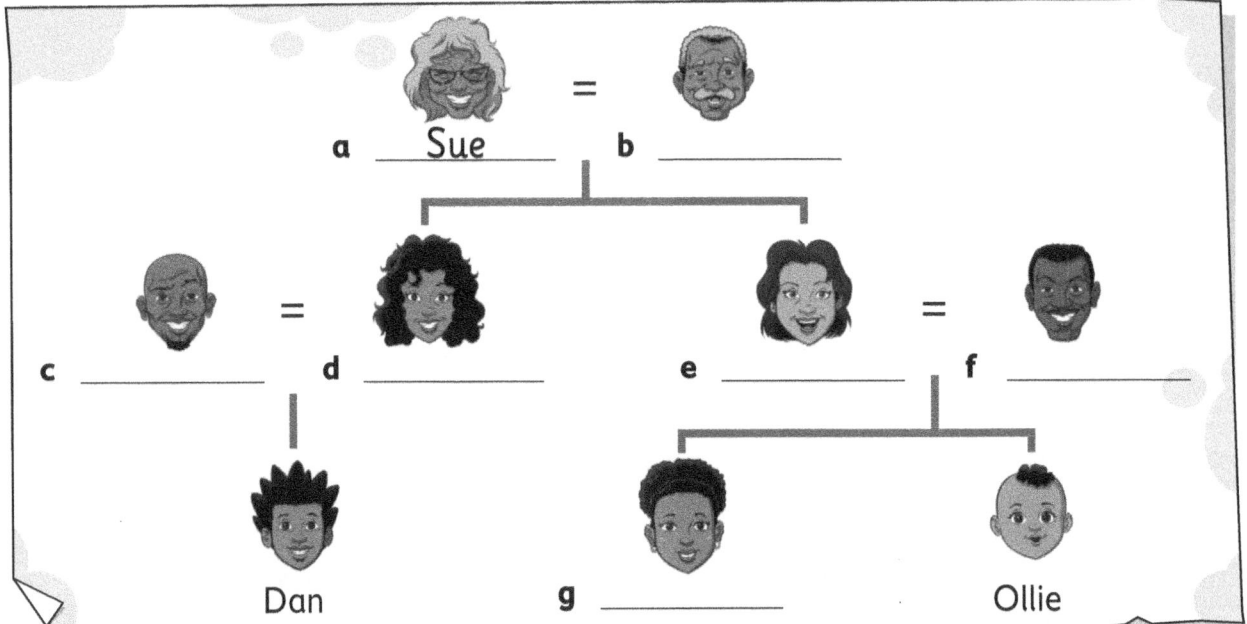

a ___Sue___   b _____

c _____   d _____   e _____   f _____

Dan   g _____   Ollie

2 **Read and write.**

1 Caroline and Andy are Ollie's ____parents____.

2 Becky is Saskia's _____.

3 Martin is Ollie's _____.

4 Dan is Saskia's _____.

5 John is Ollie's _____.

3 **Write about your family in your notebook.**

> I've got two parents. I haven't got a brother.

4 **Read and write *was* or *were*.**

1 Yesterday __was__ Dan's birthday. ✓

2 He _____ thirteen. ☐

3 The party _____ fun. ☐

4 His cousins _____ at the party. ☐

5 There _____ some games in the garden. ☐

6 He _____ wet after the games. ☐

7 There _____ a blue birthday cake. ☐

5 **Listen and tick (✓) the true sentences in Activity 4.**

6 **Look and read. Write *R* (Robbie) or *E* (Emma).**

Robbie's party in February

Emma's party in July

1 It was sunny. **E**

2 There were seven children. ☐

3 There was a big cake. ☐

4 Maddy was at the party. ☐

5 There was music. ☐

6 There were drinks. ☐

7 **What was good about the parties? Write sentences in your notebook.**

Emma's party was good because it was sunny.

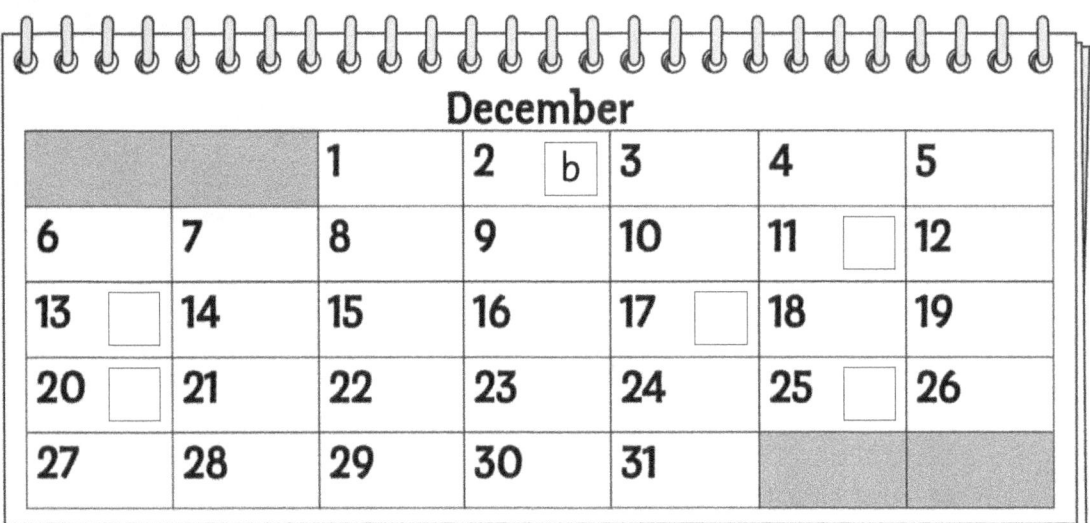

9 **Look at Activity 8. Read and write *said* or *went* and the date.**

1 Annabel __went__ to a party at school _____ on 20th December _____ .

2 She _____, 'Happy Christmas!' _____ .

3 She _____, 'Happy Birthday!' to her mum _____ .

4 She _____, 'Happy Birthday!' to her cousin _____ .

5 She _____ to her football club party _____ .

6 She _____ to a dance show _____ .

10 **Write about events from last month in your notebook.**

It was my aunt's birthday on 12th April. We went to the zoo.

11 **Look and write _ph_ or _th_. Then listen and say.**

My ¹<u>th</u>irteen___ ²bir___day was on ³___ursday.

I've got a ⁴___oto of a ⁵dol___in on my ⁶___one.

⁷Ele___ants are ⁸heal___y but they aren't very ⁹___in.

 12 **Listen and choose.**

The party was:

a at the beach.

b at school.

 13 **Listen again and complete for Lucy.**

	Lucy	Me
What was the weather like?	¹ <u>sunny</u> and ² _____	
Where was the party?	at the ³ _____	
What food was there?	⁴ _____, salad and strawberries	
What games were there?	⁵ _____	
Was there any dancing?	no	
Was there any singing?	⁶ _____	

14 **Imagine you went to a party yesterday. Complete the table in Activity 13 for you. Then write in your notebook.**

Sunday, 17th August
Yesterday, I went to a fantastic party on a boat on the river. It was hot and sunny.

15 **Number the sentences in order.**

a Polly said, 'We've got this ribbon.' ☐

b The Chief Inspector said, 'Come on, let's go.' ☐

c Smith went to Bollington Hall. 1

d Polly and Mike went to the Police Station. ☐

e The Chief Inspector said, 'Hector Frost lives at Bollington Hall.' ☐

f Smith said, 'The kids just disappeared!' ☐

16 **Read and draw.**

There was a lake near a mountain. It was snowy. There were two explorers fishing. There was a red bag behind them. There were fish in the bag. There was a polar bear on one side of the bag. There was a wolf on the other side of the bag.

17 **Imagine. What happens next in Mike and Polly's story?**

I think _____

_____ .

18 Imagine you are on the Mayflower. Circle six things for your new life.

(a doctor)	✓	horses	☐
a teacher	☐	books	☐
hens	☐	hats	☐
cows	☐	clothes	☐
pigs	☐	beds	☐

19 Listen and tick (✓) the things that were on the Mayflower.

20 Read and write. Then listen and check.

> said   was   was   went   ~~were~~   were

My Journal, by Samuel Payne

25 December 1661

Our first months here ¹ __were__ very bad. My parents
² _____ very thin because there was no food. I ³ _____
thin, too. We were very scared.

In the summer, I often ⁴ _____ to the river with my Native
American friends. I ⁵ _____ good at fishing! Then, in the
autumn, there was a big Thanksgiving party. We ⁶ _____,
'Thank you' to the Native Americans for their help.

21 Look and write the rest of Samuel's journal in your notebook.

> fifty settlers   fish from the river   'Goodbye'   meat
> ninety Native Americans   songs and games   vegetables from our farm

At the party, there were ninety Native Americans and...

22 Read and write.

Talking about the past

I ¹___was___ at a party.
You ²_____ happy.
He/She/It ³_____ great.
We ⁴_____ at school.
They ⁵_____ at the river.

There ⁶_____ a party.
There ⁷_____ some people.

I You He/She/It We They	**went** to a party. **said**, 'Hello.'

I went to the shops on my skateboard yesterday.

23 Write the missing words.

1	first	→	second	→	third	→	_fourth_
2	first	→	third	→	fifth	→	_____
3	tenth	→	fifteenth	→	twentieth	→	_____
4	third	→	tenth	→	seventeenth	→	_____
5	first	→	_____	→	twenty-first	→	thirty-first
6	thirteenth	→	tenth	→	_____	→	fourth
7	twenty-fourth	→	twelfth	→	_____	→	third
8	_____	→	fourth	→	eighth	→	sixteenth

24   **Read and choose. Then listen and check.**

Yesterday, I ¹(were / went) to a party. My favourite film stars, Keira Philips and Johnny Jones, ²(was / went) to the party, too. I ³(said / was), 'Hello.' Keira ⁴(was / were) kind and Johnny ⁵(was / were) very funny. There ⁶(was / were) some other nice people, too. We ⁷(was / were) very tired after the party but it ⁸(was / went) a fantastic day!

25   **Read and write. Then listen and check.**

cake   drinks   friends   fun   grandparents
in   was   ~~went~~   went   were

A fun party

I ¹_____went_____ to a birthday party at my school. The school ²_____ 50 years old. All of my ³_____ were there. Parents and ⁴_____ were there, too. There were a lot of ⁵_____ and food. There was a dancing competition ⁶_____ the garden, so we all ⁷_____ outside to watch. There was a big ⁸_____ from the bakery in our town. In the evening, we ⁹_____ very tired. We went home at eight o'clock. It was a ¹⁰_____ party!

26 **Write about a fun party you went to.**

_____
_____
_____
_____
_____
_____

 Are you ready for Unit 7?

7 School

1 Complete the words.

1 The first lesson at school was e _a_ _s_ y.

2 The second and third lessons were d __ __ f __ c __ __ t.

3 There was an e x __ __ t __ n __ game in the fourth lesson.

4 Lunch was b __ r __ __ g.

5 The lessons after lunch were i n __ __ r __ __ t __ __ __.

6 There was a s c __ __ __ story in the last lesson.

2 Look and write for you. Use words from Activity 1.

First Book of Words
cat
house
dog

① You: _____
Maddy: ___ _easy_ ___

PENS AND PENCILS

② You: _____
Maddy: _____

Anna and the Aliens

③ You: _____
Maddy: _____

Dinosaurs

④ You: _____
Maddy: _____

Fun with Numbers

⑤ You: _____
Maddy: _____

The Adventures of 009

⑥ You: _____
Maddy: _____

3  Listen and write for Maddy.

4 Read. Then match.

My first day at school was scary. I was only four and there were a lot of big children in the school. The lessons were very difficult. My teacher was funny but I was very sad!

1 Was Emma's first day at school scary?
2 Was she five?
3 Were there a lot of big children?
4 Were the lessons easy?
5 Was her teacher funny?
6 Was she sad?

a No, she wasn't.
b Yes, he was.
c Yes, it was.
d No, they weren't.
e Yes, she was.
f Yes, there were.

5 Find and write questions about your first day at school. Then write the answers.

1 (you) (how) (were) (old)

How old were you?

I was _____.

2 (your) (funny) (was) (teacher)

3 (the) (difficult) (lessons) (were)

4 (you) (were) (happy)

6 Write about the first time you did your favourite sport in your notebook.

- How old were you?
- Where were you?
- Was it scary/exciting/easy/difficult/relaxing?

- Who was with you?
- Were you happy?

The first time I played tennis, I was six years old. I was...

7 Find and circle six words. Then find and write the answer using the letters that aren't circled.

EGEOGRAPHYNGPESCIENCELMATHSARTISHHISTORY

What was your favourite subject last year?

E _____

8 Look and write. Then listen and choose. *True* or *false*?

✓ = was/were
✗ = wasn't/weren't

Last week...

1 ⚽ + 🌐 ✓ boring   <u>PE and Geography were boring.</u>   True / (False)

2 🌐 ✗ easy   _____   True / False

3 🎨 ✓ fun   _____   True / False

4 🔢 ✗ interesting   _____   True / False

5 🧪 + 🔢 ✗ difficult   _____   True / False

6 🎨 ✓ relaxing   _____   True / False

9 Write about your lessons last week in your notebook.

Science was fun. It was interesting, too.

 **10** Listen and read. Write the apostrophes (').

'I can't do my Science homework,' I said to my parents yesterday. 'Can you help?'
'Sorry!' said Dad. 'I havent got time. Ask your sisters.'
'They arent here,' I said.
'Your dad hasnt got time because he doesnt know the answers,' said Mum.
'He wasnt very good at Science at school. But I can help. Science is easy.'
'Thanks, Mum. This is the homework,' I said.
After a long time, Mum said, 'I dont understand. There werent any questions about those things in my Science lessons. Maybe Science isnt easy!'

 **11** Listen. Where was Suzy's school trip?

 **12** Listen again and choose.

1 Suzy's school trip was (on Thursday / yesterday).

2 There were some beautiful (statues / houses).

3 It was (an Art / a Geography) trip.

4 It was a very (interesting / boring) day.

5 The children were (excited / tired) after the trip.

6 There weren't any (buses / trains) in the afternoon.

13 Read and write about your last school trip.

My class went on a school trip (when?) _____. It was (what subject?) _____ trip. We went to (where?) _____. It was very (boring/interesting/exciting/relaxing?) _____.

14 **Look at the story and circle.**

1 (Polly / A police officer / The Chief Inspector) goes into the cave first.

2 There's a (school / tunnel / party) in the caves.

3 Polly finds (the diamonds / a key / a school timetable) in the tunnel.

4 They can't go on without a (poem / code / rope).

5 Art is at (9.00 / 10.30 / 12.40).

6 It is (morning / afternoon / night) when they come out of the tunnel.

15 **Read and tick (✔).**

1 Who is having a party?

2 Who is invited to the party?

16 **Write.**

| cave | great job | ~~party~~ | phew | tunnel |

1 There is often music at a _____party_____ .

2 A _____ is a hole in a mountain that people can go into.

3 People sometimes say '_____ _____' when you do something well.

4 A _____ can go through a mountain, underground or even under water.

5 People sometimes say '_____!' when something bad doesn't happen.

17 **Imagine. What happens next in the story?**

I think _____.

18 Look and write questions. Then answer for Tara.

1 any other children / on your farm ✗

Were there any other children on your farm?   No, there weren't.

2 any horses / on your farm ✓

_____   _____

3 a radio / in your house ✓

_____   _____

4 any teachers / near your house ✗

_____   _____

19 Listen and write.

3:19

Star Interview!

And then we went to the USA and I went to ¹____school____ there.

² _____ **you happy at your new school?**

No, I ³ _____. It was very ⁴ _____ in a class with a lot of other children.

⁵ _____ **your teachers good?**

Yes, they were. But the ⁶ _____ and English lessons were too ⁷ _____ and the History and Geography lessons were too ⁸ _____.

What was your favourite subject?

⁹ _____. I was in the basketball team. It was very ¹⁰ _____. In Australia, there ¹¹ _____ any ball sports in PE because there weren't any other children!

20 Write about your first school in your notebook.

My teacher was good. There were a lot of pictures in the classroom.

21 Read and write.

Asking about the past

Was I at school?	Yes, you [1] __were__ .	No, you **weren't**.
Were you at home?	Yes, I **was**.	No, I [2] _____.
[3] _____ he/she/it happy?	Yes, he/she/it **was**.	No, he/she/it **wasn't**.
Were we tired?	Yes, we **were**.	No, we [4] _____.
[5] _____ they funny?	Yes, they **were**.	No, they **weren't**.
Was there a cake?	Yes, there **was**.	No, there **wasn't**.
Were there any boys?	Yes, there **were**.	No, there **weren't**.

Talking about the past (negative)

I [6] _____ at the party.
You **weren't** in the kitchen.
He/She/It **wasn't** scary.
We [7] _____ on TV.
They **weren't** sad.

There **wasn't** a cat.
There **weren't** any dogs.

Was I good at Music at school?

Er, yes, dear.

22 Read and write. Then listen and check.

> was (x 3)   wasn't   were (x 2)   weren't

Interviewer: What was your school like, David?

David: My school [1] ___was___ a tennis school.

Interviewer: Were there other lessons, too?

David: Yes, there [2] _____ – Maths, Science, English and History.
But they [3] _____ only in the morning. There were tennis lessons every afternoon.

Interviewer: [4] _____ it a good school?

David: Yes, it [5] _____. My sister [6] _____ happy there.
Her favourite subject was Art but there [7] _____ any Art teachers at the school. But it was a great school for a tennis player!

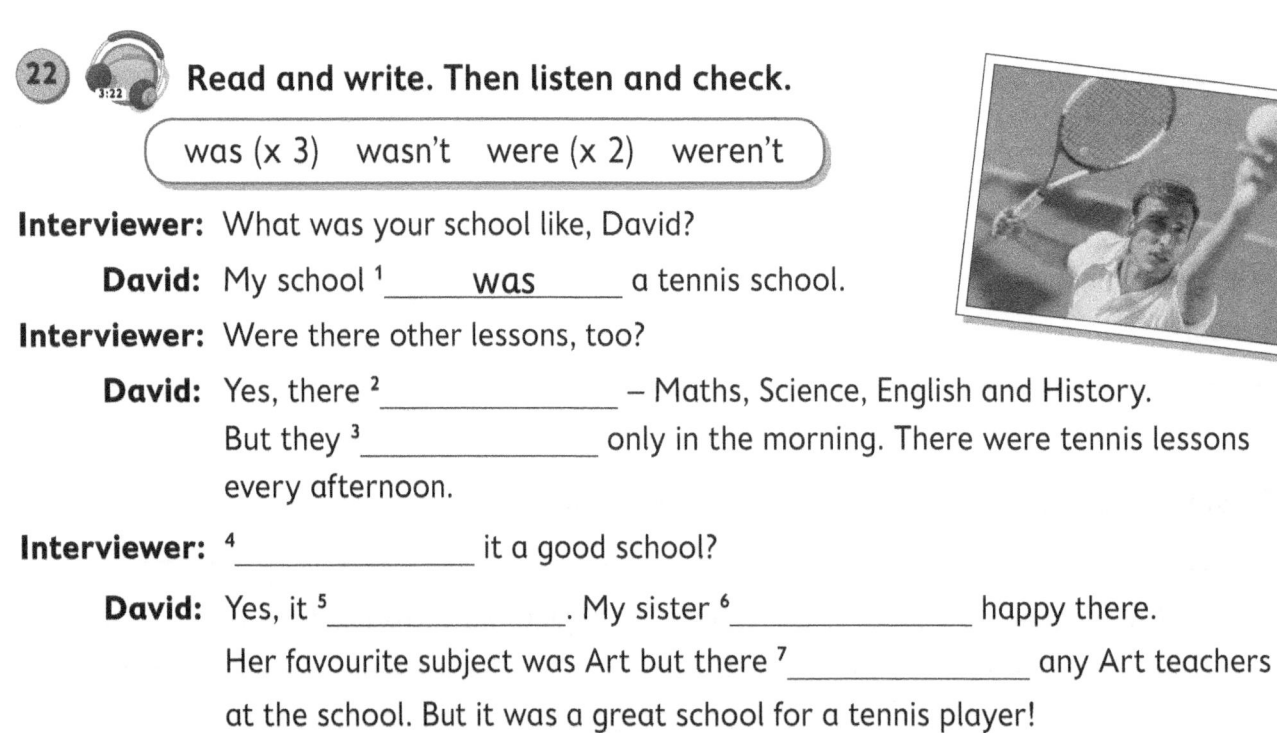

23 **Read and write. Then listen and check.**

> because   difficult   easy   English   exciting
> favourite   interesting   PE   ~~Science~~   was

My favourite subjects last year

My favourite subjects last year were English, PE and ¹___Science___ .
²_____ was good because there were a lot of ³_____ stories
for us to read. Science was ⁴_____ but the teacher ⁵_____
very good. Her classes were ⁶_____ . She's my favourite teacher.
⁷_____ was fun ⁸_____ I'm good at sports. Wednesday was
my ⁹_____ day because we played sports all afternoon. PE was
¹⁰_____ because there were no tests.

24 **Write about your favourite subjects last year. Use:** *(Maths) was/wasn't...*

_____

_____

_____

_____

_____

_____

_____

_____

_____

_____

_____

_____

 Are you ready for Unit 8?

8 Entertainment

1 Write the nationalities in the crossword.

1	the USA →	<u>American</u>
2	Mexico →	_____
3	Spain →	_____
4	China →	_____
5	Britain →	_____
6	Argentina →	_____
7	Australia →	_____
8	Italy →	_____
9	Egypt →	_____
10	Brazil →	_____

¹A ²m e r i c a n

2 Listen and match.

1	Nicole Kidman	Spain	football player
2	J.K. Rowling	Australia	writer
3	Rafael Nadal	the USA	singer
4	Lionel Messi	Argentina	tennis player
5	Beyoncé	Britain	actress

3 Write about the people in Activity 2 in your notebook.

1 Nicole Kidman is an Australian actress.

4 **Read and write the years in numbers and in words.**

1 Last year, it was ___2016___ (_____twenty sixteen_____).

2 Two years ago, it was _____ (_____).

3 Ten years ago, it was _____ (_____).

4 Fifty years ago, it was _____ (_____).

5 🎧 **Listen and write.**

> Name: **Pharrell Williams**
> Nationality: American
> Job: singer, actor and TV star
> ¹ _2009_ : first TV programme
> ² _____ : first film
> ³ _____ : first music for a film
> ⁴ _____ : first singing competition on TV

Pharrell Williams

6 **Imagine you are famous and write.**

> Name: _____
> Nationality: _____
> Job: _____
> 2015: _____
> 2028: _____
> 2029: _____
> 1st October 2030: _____
> 24th November 2030: _____

7 **Look at Activity 6. Imagine it is 1st December 2030. Write sentences using *last* or *ago* in your notebook.**

> Last week, I went to China.
> Two years ago, I was in my first Real Madrid match.

8 Find and circle. Then write.

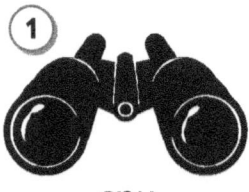

1   spy

c	o	w	b	o	y	s	w	o	i	h
d	s	a	b	t	e	a	c	h	e	r
e	o	i	u	j	r	k	c	j	i	s
y	l	t	n	s	a	i	l	o	r	p
q	d	e	l	d	a	n	c	e	r	y
f	i	r	e	f	i	g	h	t	e	r
u	e	s	f	a	c	t	o	r	f	n
l	r	a	s	t	r	o	n	a	u	t
s	c	i	e	n	t	i	s	t	x	n

2

3

4

5

6

7

8

9

10

11

12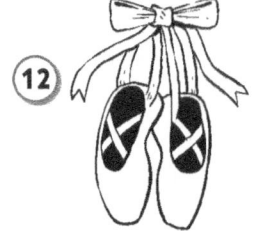

9 Look and write.

> 1995   25th August   December   half past three   night
> Saturday   seven o'clock   the afternoon   the winter   Tuesday

in	on	at
1995		

10  **Read and write. Then listen, check and say.**

1 A _____swimmer_____ can swim.

2 A _____ can dance.

3 An actor can _____.

4 A _____ can sail.

5 A _____ can sing.

6 A teacher can _____.

11 **Read. Then listen and number.**

TV Today!

a ☐ **7.30 The Chat Show**
Steve Kilmer talks to young film star, Ethan Davis.

b ☐ **8.00 Today in Sport**
All the big matches: football, basketball, tennis!

c ☐ **9.00 The Island**
Twelve people are living together on a small island. Life isn't easy!

Tuesday 10th August

12 **Listen again and write.**

1 The tennis match is very ____exciting____.

2 The players in the match are Spanish and _____.

3 The film star was a _____ in his first film.

4 The film star's birthday was _____ weeks ago.

5 On the island, there isn't any _____.

6 There was rain on the island three _____ ago.

13 **Write about your favourite TV or radio programme in your notebook.**

Clever Treasure
Channel 1 at 6.30 p.m. on Tuesdays
The pirates in this exciting story are...

14 **Look at the story and match.**

1 How does the Queen feel?   **a** The Chief Inspector.

2 What does Mike do?   **b** The Queen.

3 How do Frost and Smith feel?   **c** She is amused and surprised.

4 Who says, 'How extraordinary!'   **d** He finds the diamonds.

5 Where are the diamonds?   **e** They feel angry and scared.

6 Who says, 'Quick! Catch them!'   **f** They're in the ice wall.

15 **Draw your favourite character and write a description.**

1 My favourite character is _____.

2 He/She's got _____.

3 He/She is _____.

4 He/She likes _____.

16 **Imagine. What happens next to the characters?**

I think _____.

17  **Read and circle. Then listen and check.**

¹(In / On / At) the winter, it's dark after school. I come home ²(in / on / at) half past three and do my homework. Then, I play computer games. ³(Last / Yesterday / Three) year, my favourite computer game was *Nintendogs* but now my favourite is *Guitar Hero.* Two months ⁴(last / ago / then), I wasn't very good at ⁵(play / player / playing) the game – some of the music is very difficult – but now I'm a good ⁶(play / player / playing). I often play ⁷(in / on / at) the evening with my friends and ⁸(in / on / at) Saturdays and Sundays, too.

18 **Read the puzzle and think.**

Four days ago, a cowboy went to the city on Friday.
Yesterday, he went home on Friday. How?

19 **Read and circle.** *True (✓)* or *false (✗)?* **Then find and write the answer.**

Technology Quiz...

		✓	✗
1	There were computer games one hundred years ago.	✔ We	✗ The
2	There were computer games in 1940.	✔ can	✗ horse's
3	Mario is a famous computer game character.	✔ name	✗ act
4	Before the books and films, Harry Potter was a computer game.	✔ in	✗ was
5	In FIFA computer games, you play football.	✔ Friday	✗ films

1   <u>The</u>   2   _____   3   _____

4   _____   5   _____!

20 Read and write.

Talking about times

1 last	week month year	**2 _____**	two days six months ten years

3 _____	January the summer 1979	**4 _____**	Thursday 1st February	**5 _____**	night half past eight

Two weeks ago, I was on TV!

21 Read and write in a different way.

1 His film was very successful in 2010. (It's now 2011.)

<u>His film was very successful last year.</u>

2 That was my favourite computer game in July. (It's now September.)

_____

3 The programme was on TV two days ago. (It's now Wednesday.)

_____

4 She was on the radio on 2nd February. (It's now 9th February.)

_____

5 My dad was a singer twelve years ago. (It's now 2015.)

_____

6 We were in Hollywood three months ago. (It's now November.)

_____

7 I went to the supermarket yesterday. (It's now 5th July.)

_____

8 Steve went to bed two hours ago. (It's now eleven o'clock.)

_____

22 **Read and write. Then listen and check.**

| actor | American | English | film | friends |
| home | listen | music | sports | ~~watching~~ |

My favourite entertainment

○ My favourite kind of entertainment is ¹ __watching__ TV. I love watching films at
² _____. I often watch one ³ _____ many times. I like watching
films in ⁴ _____. My favourite ⁵ _____ is Robert Pattinson
because he's good-looking. I ⁶ _____ to music, too. I download
⁷ _____ from the internet. I love ⁸ _____ music. I like playing
○ many ⁹ _____ and often play with my ¹⁰ _____ in the park.

23 **Write about your favourite entertainment.**

_____
_____
_____
_____
_____
_____
_____
_____
_____
_____
_____
_____
_____

1 Write.

1 Who are the Ice Detectives? <u>Mike and Polly.</u>

2 Where are the thieves now? _____

3 What do the children and Gizmo eat to celebrate? _____

4 Who has got a new pet? _____

5 How do you know that the Queen remembers Mike and Polly? _____

6 How do the explorers know that Mike and Polly found the diamonds? _____

2 Circle.

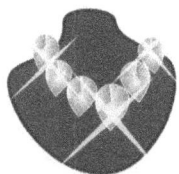

1 Whose is this?
It's (Hector Frost's / (the Queen's)).

2 Where did Hector Frost first see it?
He saw it (on TV / in town).

3 Who used these?
(Smith / Hector Frost) used them.

4 What did he see through them?
He saw (a polar bear / Mike and Polly).

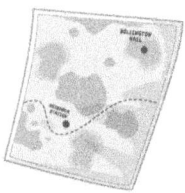

5 Who had this on the mountain?
(The explorers / Mike and Polly) had it on the mountain.

6 What did they use it for?
They used it for following (the road / Smith).

7 Whose are these?
They're (Mike's / Smith's).

8 Where did he use them?
He used them at (the training camp / Bollington Hall).

Thanksgiving

1 Complete the crossword.

Across: 2, 5
Down: 1 p u m p k i n p i e

5 m _ r _ _ _ _ _ _ _ _ _ _ _

2 Read and tick (✓). Then listen and check.

1 Thanksgiving is in:

 a □  b ✓

2 Children don't go to school on:

 a □  b □

3 Charlie plays the:

 a □  b □

4 People usually eat:

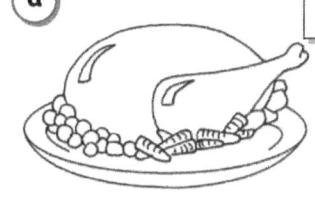 a □  b □

Wordlist

1
Friends

- artist
- bald
- beautiful
- bossy
- clever
- cool
- cute
- good-looking
- handsome
- kind
- lazy
- shy
- spiky
- sporty
- straight
- thieves
- warm

What **does** she
  look like?
What **do** they
  look like?
She**'s**/They**'re**
  beautiful.
She**'s**/They**'ve got**
  blond hair.
You're sporty **and**
  you're clever.
You're bossy **but**
  I don't mind.
I like you **because**
  you're kind.

2
My life

- after
- afternoon
- always
- before
- be on time
- bones
- brush my teeth
- do my homework
- evening
- igloo
- make my bed
- meet my friends
- never
- ribbons
- often
- sometimes
- take notes in class
- tidy my room
- usually
- wash my face

He does **his**
  homework.
She washes **her**
  face.
It washes **its** head.
We brush **our**
  teeth.
They brush **their**
  hair.
My sister**'s** kite

3
Free time

- acting
- catching
- climbing
- diving
- drawing
- hitting
- instruments
- kicking
- piano
- playing chess
- playing the drums
- rollerblading
- running races
- skateboarding
- throwing
- tracks
- trampolining
- trumpet
- violins
- wolf

I**'m**/You**'re** good
  at throw**ing**.
She **isn't good at**
  danc**ing**.
They **aren't good**
  at climb**ing**.
What do you **like**
  do**ing**?
What **are** you
  good at?
He/She **loves**
  skateboard**ing**.
They **like** act**ing**.

4
Around the world

- Argentina
- Australia
- Brazil
- Britain
- cave
- China
- city
- desert
- Egypt
- forest
- Greenland
- Italy
- lake
- Mexico
- pyramid
- Spain
- statue
- the USA
- volcano

There**'s a**
  competition.
There **isn't a**
  competition.
There **are some**/
  aren't any
  snakes.
Is there **a** desert?
Are there **any**
  volcanoes?
Yes, there **is/are**.
No, there **isn't**/
  aren't.

5
Shopping

baggy
bend
cheap
dark
expensive
gloves
jacket
light
middle
pounds
rock climbing
sandals
scarf
soft
soles
stiff
sunglasses
swimsuit
tight
umbrella
wallet

How much is that
  scarf?
It's two pounds
  fifty.
How much are
  those gloves?
They're fifteen
  pounds.
Can I buy this
  jacket, please?
It**'s**/They**'re too**
  expensive.

6
Party time

aunt
baby
cousin
granny
grandad
grandparents
Native Americans
North America
parents
party
polar bear
settlers
Thanksgiving
uncle

first   eleventh
second   twelfth
third   thirteenth
fourth   fourteenth
fifth   fifteenth
sixth   sixteenth
seventh seventeenth
eighth   eighteenth
ninth   nineteenth
tenth   twentieth
             twenty-first

I **was** very hungry.
The cars **were**
  small.
I **said**, 'Happy
  New Year!'
I **went** to a party.

7
School

Art
boring
difficult
easy
exciting
funny
Geography
interesting
kilometres
Maths
PE
History
radio
relaxing
scary
Science

Was it scary?
Yes, it **was**./No, it
  wasn't.
Were they the
  winners?
Yes, they **were**./
No, they **weren't**.
Was there an
  alien in it?
Yes, there **was**./
No, there **wasn't**.
Were there any
  children in the
  story?
Yes, there **were**./
No, there **weren't**.
Last year, Maths
  wasn't easy.
The lessons
  weren't fun.

8
Entertainment

American
Argentinian
Australian
autograph
Brazilian
British
Chinese
cowboy
Egyptian
Italian
Japanese
king
Mexican
sailor
scientist
soldier
Spanish
spy
successful
table tennis
waiter

She was in a film
  two days **ago**.
He was in a
  Spanish team **last**
  week.
in the morning
on Thursday
at five o'clock

Families of the world

help
husband

Funny sports

cheese rolling
elephant polo
hill
mud racing
reindeer racing
sticks
winner

Shopping for food

bakery
coconuts
floating
grow
seeds

Unusual schools

boarding school
international
Japanese
skier
snowboarding
the Olympics

Festival

Thanksgiving

American football
colourful
mashed potato
parade
pumpkin pie
trumpet
turkey